D-STRESS

Building Resilience in Challenging Times

7 Simple Techniques

MEIRON LEES

First published in 2008
www.meironlees.com.au

Copyright © Meiron Lees 2008
The moral rights of the author have been asserted.

This work is copyright.
Apart from any use as permitted under the *Copyright Act 1968*, no part may be reproduced, copied, scanned, stored in a retrieval system, recorded, or transmitted, in any form or by any means, without the prior written permission of the publisher.

Cover design & book design by Ful-vue
www.ful-vue.com

> Lees, Meiron, 1966-
>
> D-stress : building resilience in challenging times
> 7 simple techniques / Meiron Lees.
>
> 2nd Edition
>
> ISBN 978-1-925049-15-2
>
> Stress management.

Disclaimer
The information in this book is not intended as a substitute for professional medical advice and treatment. If you are suffering from any medical conditions or health problems, it is recommended that you consult a medical professional before following any of the advice or practice suggested in this book. The author, publisher or any other persons involved in working on this publication cannot accept responsibility for any injuries or damage as a result of following the information, techniques or advice contained in this book.

Dedication

Dedicated with love to my parents
Zelda and Sender

Acknowledgements

It is with gratitude and appreciation that I give thanks to the wonderful people that have supported, encouraged and assisted me along the journey in making *D-Stress* a reality.

To my parents, Sender and Zelda who shower me with love, empowerment and care, unwaveringly believe in my passion and purpose and touch me with their selfless commitment to my life journey. No words can describe my deep sense of gratitude.

Anabel and Sol, I thank you both sincerely for your infectious exuberance of positivity and enthusiasm. Your skill, professionalism and heart fill this book with your wonderful energy.

I would like to give thanks to Gerald Camberg, my friend and mentor who so generously gives of his wisdom, time and energy.

And finally to you, the reader, my teacher who I give thanks for through writing this book, it has given me the opportunity to constantly remind myself of my purpose to live with peace of mind and serenity and to embrace the feeling of joy and contentment.

Contents

10	**Section 1** Introduction
20	**Section 2** What causes us to feel stressed?
28	**Section 3** 7 resilience builders to manage your stress
32	**Resilience Builder 1:** Transforming your Thought Attacks™
40	**Resilience Builder 2:** Asking the right questions
46	**Resilience Builder 3:** Focusing on the now
52	**Resilience Builder 4:** Telling a different story
62	**Resilience Builder 5:** Changing the labels
68	**Resilience Builder 6:** Observing the feeling
74	**Resilience Builder 7:** Developing a sense of gratitude
82	**Section 4** A final word
86	Quick reference: *D-Stress* Resilience Builders
91	Bibliography
96	**Section 5** Stress health check

section 01

Introduction

My life in South Africa

It was 1998 and I was living in Johannesburg, South Africa. The city had just received the rather unfortunate honour of being the crime capital of the world but this was my home and these were my circumstances. On a daily basis I was surrounded by violence: carjackings, armed robberies and muggings were all part of daily life.

I lived in a modest house in the suburbs but it was different to what would usually be considered a home. It was like a prison, surrounded by a wall on which a high voltage electric fence towered over the street below. It was my warning to others that this property was out of bounds.

I lived in fear. I was on constant watch at all times and alert to any suspicious person that could potentially do me harm. Driving was particularly stressful as most carjackings occurred when vehicles were stationery at traffic lights.

There were few who remained unaffected. While I had been lucky, my parents and sister had all suffered traumatic experiences at the mercy of ruthless carjackers aimlessly waving their guns like some sort of victory salute. I was fortunate not to have fallen prey to the violent crime that my family, friends and colleagues had experienced.

One Saturday evening it was my turn to fully appreciate what many others had endured.

I was driving home at about 11:30pm after a dinner party with friends and was stationery at a red light in a neighbouring suburb when a loud smashing noise reverberated through me.

My heart started pounding and I was terrified and confused. Was I being carjacked? Was I being shot at? What was going on?

I noticed a hand reaching through my shattered car window in the direction of my mobile phone resting on its cradle. Instinctively I grabbed hold of this intrusive arm in an absurd attempt to rescue something that was by no means worth my life. In a flash the hand was gone, as was my mobile phone.

I checked to see if I was OK. Had I been shot? Had I been hurt by the shower of thousands of pieces of glass that rained down on me? I sat feeling terrified yet grateful when I realised that my fate was not worse than others I knew so well.

Just a few months earlier a friend had lost his life in a bid to save his utility vehicle. Another had died in an attempt to reclaim his mobile phone from a murderous thief.

I was in shock, but I was alive.

My challenge

My life was stressful but I was determined not to allow these events to destroy the quality of my life by living with fear, anxiety and stress.

In an attempt to find the answer to living a calm and peaceful life in the midst of extreme circumstances I began my journey. But before I could start there was something I needed to admit to myself.

I had never admitted that I didn't quite have the skills to effectively manage my day to day stress yet alone manage living in a high stress environment. I was now ready to admit this weakness and to find the way to become resilient to life's challenges.

This was my goal and I longed to feel a sense of calm and contentment. I wanted to find a way to live with peace of mind and inner stability.

At times I felt guilty that I didn't feel better about my life: I had a good job, a beautiful home and was surrounded by caring and supportive family and friends. My life was great on the outside but inside I simply wasn't fulfilled.

I kept blaming my environment for my stressful feelings and lack of happiness even though I knew that it was up to me to change it. I thought I could try and trick myself into believing that everything was fine and that I should think positively all the time but it wasn't that simple.

I started to recall the words of a motivational speaker I had once heard:

When life gives you lemons, make lemonade.

I thought:
That's easy for you to say, but how do I do it? How do I control these thoughts that churn through my mind and cause me to feel stressed?

I knew there had to be a way I could change these thoughts that were sabotaging my feelings of contentment and happiness.

I had become aware when talking to people that the majority were quite negative when they spoke about their lives. I rarely found someone who had a positive outlook, especially when they were faced with challenges.

I pondered on why we seem to immediately default to seeing the glass as half empty. Why weren't we all walking around with smiles on our faces, thinking positively?

I was convinced that life was not just about overcoming difficulties but about living a more fulfilled and contented existence.

> I knew there had to be a way I could change these thoughts that were sabotaging my feelings of contentment and happiness.

- I wasn't going to stop until I found a way to reach my goal.
- I was no longer prepared to allow people or situations to determine the way I felt.
- I would no longer tolerate feeling controlled by my circumstances.
- I would no longer be a victim of life's seemingly cruel intentions.

Pursuing the goal

I travelled both nationally and internationally seeking those that could teach me to live with peace of mind and resilience. I consulted historical teachings and spent hours consciously reflecting on how I could live a life where I was the master of my mind.

I was hungry to find the freedom of choosing my own emotional state rather than allowing situations or people to influence how I felt. The process of the pursuit was challenging but I kept practising the teachings I learned.

At times I felt great frustration and disappointment when I still reacted in the same way. I felt stressed when things didn't go well for me but I knew that I had to persist if I was to master the way I felt instead of relinquishing my feelings to others or life's situations.

I had to stay focused on this goal; it would be the deciding factor between fulfilment and discontentment.

I imagined a life where, no matter what happened, I could still choose my state of mind and emotions. Even if a situation was less than ideal I didn't want to give it the power to control me. I knew it would be worth all the pain to reach my goal, or to even get close to the ideal. I was determined and committed so I continued practising the techniques I learned and slowly began to see some changes.

I noticed that I had become less affected by the violence that surrounded me. I had started to think differently about my life and my stress and fear began to fall away.

I also noticed my perspective towards my relationships and life's difficulties seemed less threatening to my emotional state than ever before. Able to see the change in my life I kept applying the techniques and strategies I knew I could depend upon when life presented its challenges.

My intentions for writing this book

I have written this book in response to the increasing incidence of stress in our contemporary culture and to show you that the possibility of peace, clarity and emotional stability is realistic and attainable.

I know it's possible because these techniques and strategies have supported and sustained me when I've faced life's problems and uncertainties and help me to this day.

I have endeavoured to write this book in a way that is both practical and relevant. Some of the concepts and techniques may be new to you at first but with practise and commitment they will soon become your everyday tools by which you can manage your stress.

This book will give you practical and user-friendly ways to *D-Stress*. You won't have to wade through countless pages to find out how to apply the techniques. They're explained simply and use examples that relate to everyday living.

I encourage you to start by choosing one technique and practising it for 21 days. After this time you'll find it has become a habit. When it does you'll start to feel a sense of lightness and optimism.

I have been using these techniques for many years now and they have helped me control my thoughts and create a better quality of life. I've also found the fulfilment inside that I had been searching for.

I hope you find comfort and support in the pages that follow and that these techniques enable you to realise the goal we all share.

With warm wishes,

Meiron

Meiron Lees

section 02

What causes us to feel stressed?

The notion of stress is extremely subjective; what may be stressful to one person may not seem stressful to another.

What is important is that most of the stress we feel, regardless of what causes it, is harmful.

If we can reduce it we'll not only live happier, healthier and more contented lives, we'll also be able to carry out our work with more focus, performing closer to our highest potential.

So what causes us to feel stressed?

We often feel stressed in a situation when we are not in control of the outcome or when we feel that we have little or no option available to change it.

Here's an example to illustrate this:

Mike, a business owner, is about to board a train to a client meeting where they will make their final decision whether or not to sign his proposed $1,000,000 contract.

Business has been tough for Mike and this contract could determine whether he continues with his own business or starts applying for employment. He has been working day and night for months on the proposal and there's a lot at stake. Two senior executives have flown in from out-of-town and he has been told that the meeting can be no longer than an hour long. The arrival time for the train approaches and an announcement is made informing passengers that the train has been delayed by 20 minutes. Mike realises that he will never make his meeting on time and begins to feel extremely stressed.

Mike's stress is caused by the fact that he feels he has no control over the arrival of the train. He feels he has limited options at his disposal to resolve the problem.

We often believe that the events in our lives are responsible for our feelings of stress and that our circumstances determine the way we feel.

To challenge this notion picture this:

You are driving down the street and someone speeds past and cuts you off. You may think to yourself: What an idiot! How dare they drive so dangerously? They should be taken off the road! *You may even start to feel angry at this person, curse them or stretch out a finger or two.*

If I stopped you at this point and asked you why you were feeling so worked up you might say:

This idiot just cut me off!
How else would you like me to feel?
I almost had an accident!

This is a good example of how situations can determine the way you feel. A reckless driver caused you to feel angry and stressed and you have allowed yourself to become a victim to the actions of others.

Why are you placing your feelings at their mercy? When do the situations or actions of others stop becoming the cause for the way you feel and at what point do you start to take control of your feelings and emotions?

The answers to these questions lie in your understanding of how your feelings and emotions come about.

The process most often works like this:

Process

Event | We experience an event, a situation or circumstance.

▼

Thought | We then have a thought about the event.

▼

Emotion | We then experience a feeling from the thought.

Let's use our driving example to see how it fits into the **event ▸ thought ▸ emotion** process: ▸

Event | *You are driving and someone cuts you off.*
▼
Thought | *You think: This person should be taken off the road.*
▼
Emotion | *You start to feel angry.*

Now think about this:
Your thoughts about a situation determine the way you feel.

Let's continue our driving story.

A few kilometres down the road our reckless driver does the same thing to someone else. That person gets a fright but thinks: Thank goodness they didn't crash into me! I hope there is no emergency that has caused this person to be in such a dreadful rush. *She continues her journey feeling grateful and appreciative that she wasn't harmed and feels a sense of compassion for the driver.*

Let's think about these two events for a moment.

Both people have experienced the same event but have had two very different responses. What was the reason for these different responses? What made one person respond with anger and the other with appreciation and compassion?

It wasn't the event itself, otherwise they both would have had the same response. What differed were the thoughts they had about the event. One had thoughts that fuelled anger while the other had thoughts that generated gratitude.

It was the choice of thought that made the difference to the way they felt.

Your thoughts about a situation determine the way you feel.

So how does stress relate to your choices of thought?

Stress is a feeling and what causes that feeling is what you're thinking. Generally, you don't have a stressful feeling without first having a stressful thought. But why do you have stressful thoughts in the first place? Why can't we just think happy and positive thoughts all the time?

To know the answers to these questions you first need to understand a little bit about the mind and how it works. Here is an interesting fact. Every day you think approximately 60,000 thoughts. That's 60,000 bits of information, ideas, opinions, judgements and beliefs streaming through your mind every day.

Amazingly, about 90% of these thoughts are the same thoughts you had yesterday. So that's about 54,000 of the same thoughts flowing through your mind every day. (And we wonder why it's difficult to create new ideas!) Even more interesting is that most of these 54,000 thoughts are negative in nature.

So let's recap:
You have about 60,000 thoughts each day. 90% of these thoughts are the same as the ones you had yesterday and the majority of them are negative.

No wonder it's so challenging for us to remain positive and keep our stressful thoughts at bay! So how can we manage and control our thoughts so that we sponsor positive emotions and limit the stress caused by our negative thoughts?

The next section will provide the answers.

section 03

7 resilience builders
to manage your stress

In this section you will learn 7 techniques to help you manage and reduce your stress.

Resilience Builder 1: Transforming your Thought Attacks™

Resilience Builder 2: Asking the right questions

Resilience Builder 3: Focusing on the now

Resilience Builder 4: Telling a different story

Resilience Builder 5: Changing the labels

Resilience Builder 6: Observing the feeling

Resilience Builder 7: Developing a sense of gratitude

Each of these resilience builders can be immediately applied to any stressful situation that you are experiencing. I have chosen these techniques as they have helped me to manage and reduce my own stress, regardless of the situation.

I will share my personal experiences and show you how I have applied them in the stressful situations I have come across in my life.

After you have read all 7 techniques, pause for a moment and see if any of them stand out from the rest or if you feel attracted to any one in particular. It's important to focus on one technique to start with.

> **After practising the technique for 21 days you'll start to create a new pattern of thinking.**

Once you've chosen your technique follow these 3 simple steps.

Step 1 | Reread the technique you've chosen to master.

Step 2 | Think about a situation that is currently causing you to feel stressed.

Step 3 | Apply the technique to the stressful situation.

Practise the technique for at least 21 consecutive days and make a commitment to apply it whenever you start feeling stressed. After practising the technique for 21 days you'll start to create a new pattern of thinking in your mind. This pattern will eventually become your default thinking habit whenever you're faced with challenging circumstances. It will help prevent you from falling into the stress trap you previously created.

It's important that you continue to practise the technique every time you start to feel stressed. It's like exercising any muscle in your body, once you've toned it you need to keep working out to keep it strong and healthy.

During your practise you may get frustrated. This can happen when you're faced with a stressful situation and respond in exactly the same way you did before. Please don't be put off! It's normal to continue to do what you've been doing for years. Remember that you're breaking a lifelong habit and that takes time. Change is never instantaneous so be patient and kind to yourself and the results will show.

After a few months of frequent and continuous practise you will notice that you start to respond differently to situations that would have caused you to feel stressed in the past. This will be the indicator that the technique is working.

Keep the book handy and read it anytime you feel you need a reminder of how to maintain control of your stressful feelings.

With these techniques, it's my intention to help you enjoy a truly joyful and contented life.

Change is never
instantaneous
so be patient and
kind to yourself
and the results
will show.

Resilience Builder 1:
Transforming your Thought Attacks™

We have learned from the previous section that one of the main causes of stress is the way you think about a particular situation, not the situation itself. These thoughts act as a lens through which you give meaning to your life and interpret it.

A Thought Attack™ is what happens when your mind turns on itself and attacks any possibility of a positive outlook. It does this by focusing your thoughts on the negative and threatening aspects of a situation.

Once a Thought Attack™ enters your mind it starts to attract similar thoughts and begins to snowball. It gains further momentum until feelings of stress, anxiety and panic set in.

When you experience Thought Attacks™ you have given permission for negative thoughts to have free reign in your mind and consequently allowed feelings of stress to enter your body.

Thought Attacks™ are the biggest threat known to mankind. They infect us all many times a day and affect us in ways we don't even realise causing illness, poor health, low self-esteem and unhappiness. On a larger scale, they can result in intolerance, hatred, violence and conflict.

So what happens when we experience a Thought Attack™?

This example will help explain:

You decide to enter a 100km cycling race. You have completed a few of these races before but you've never reached your goal of finishing the race in under 3 hours. Everyday for months you wake up early to train. You're committed and disciplined. You even lose a few kilograms and go to bed early so that you'll be fresh for each morning's training session.

The day finally arrives. The gun goes off and away you go. You're feeling strong and positive. The race is going well until you suddenly hit a pot-hole and fall off your bicycle onto the road. Your skin is scraped and bruised but you can still continue the race. You check the damage to your bicycle and discover a tyre puncture. By the time you've cleaned up and repaired the tyre 20 minutes have gone by and you realise that you'll never finish the race within your goal time.

I'm sure you'll agree this event has the potential to cause a little stress!

So how can you respond?

Response 1:
Thought Attack™ Response
(Usual default thinking)

While you're busy repairing your tyre thoughts start to churn inside your head.

You think to yourself:

I can't believe this has happened! I'm such an idiot I should have seen the pot-hole. What a waste of all that training! Why don't tyre companies make decent tyres that don't puncture so easily? Why is life so unfair? Why did this happen to me?

When you choose responses like this you're experiencing a Thought Attack™!

So what can you do to overcome it and what's the antidote that would make you feel more positive and less stressed?

Let's look at what another response to this situation could look like.

Response 2:
The Wise Owl Response
(*D-Stress* way of thinking)

While you're repairing your tyre you think:

Thankfully I'm only slightly injured. I hit the pot-hole at 30km an hour and could have been badly hurt. I can still finish the race but that's not much of a challenge for me. What other goal can I set so that I can feel that I've achieved something?

You decide to reset a new time and challenge yourself to ride at an even faster pace. With this thought in mind you regain your feeling of excitement about the race and don't allow the situation to sabotage your positive state of mind.

The Wise Owl Response is valuable because it helps you view life's challenging situations in a way that benefit you rather than allowing them to create feelings of stress or depression.

Why do we often default to Thought Attack™ responses rather than to Wise Owl Responses?

The reason is simple and obvious. We haven't been taught how to think!

Thinking is a technique, an art and a learned skill which requires practise. Without relearning or developing your thinking it's very difficult to face challenges, particularly when you don't have the tools to overcome them. How can a soldier fight a battle without adequate protection or armour?

If we think back to the majority of our thoughts being negative it's no wonder that leaving the mind to its own accord automatically defaults it to thinking negatively!

The most important thing to appreciate is that in every situation, whether you're aware of it or not, you can choose an interpretation of how you perceive the situation to be.

If your interpretation is pessimistic you're likely to feel apprehension, anxiety or stress. If your interpretation is optimistic you'll promote feelings of positivity, excitement and joy. Unfortunately when you've had many repeated, challenging experiences it's easy to adopt a negative interpretation. Just remember, you always have a choice if you remain consciously aware of your thinking patterns.

Changing the way you interpret challenging situations is what will transform a potentially stressful event into one that could produce a benefit or positive emotion. By choosing The Wise Owl Response the possibility of stress reduces dramatically.

So how do you become conscious of your Thought Attacks™?

The answer is the Red Card.

In a football game, a referee will often pull out a Red Card from his pocket and send a player off the field. Why do they do this? The referee has deemed the player's actions to be so negative and damaging that the player is sent off the field to cool down.

So how do we use the Red Card against our Thought Attacks™? Whenever you feel a Thought Attack™ coming on give yourself a Red Card and follow these three points:

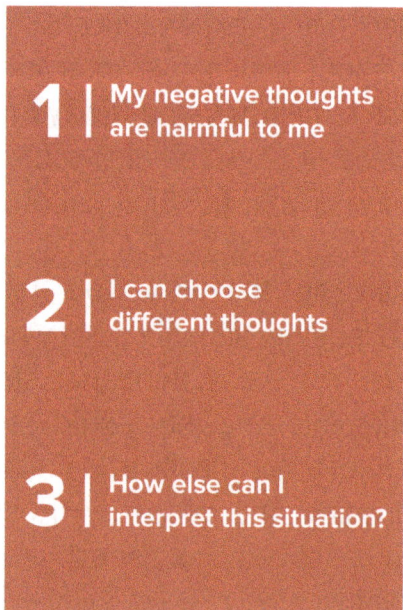

1 | My negative thoughts are harmful to me

2 | I can choose different thoughts

3 | How else can I interpret this situation?

1. My negative thoughts are harmful to me.

The first point on the Red Card is to remind you that your Thought Attacks™ are harmful. They prevent you from feeling confident, empowered and positive. They have the power to turn you into the victim of your situation, leaving you at the mercy of others and your circumstances.

2. I can choose different thoughts.

The second point acts as a reminder that you have the ability to choose which thoughts to focus on and which to discard. It's difficult to stop the barrage of negative thoughts that enter your mind, especially when it seems as though it's just happening to you and out of your control. Always remember that you can choose which to hold on to and which to let go. Become intolerant in allowing your Thought Attacks™ to stay in your head!

Thought Attacks™ are only harmful for as long as they stay in your mind so the longer you keep them there, the more stressed you'll become.

Remember that you're the one in control of where you would like to focus your attention.

By choosing supportive thoughts you give yourself a better chance to make the most out of something that could cause you stress.

3. How else can I interpret this situation?

The last point on the Red Card is a question that, when answered, can transform your Thought Attacks™ immediately. In asking how else you could interpret a stressful situation, your mind begins to seek an alternative way of viewing the situation and your focus changes towards a new perspective. This new way of looking at the situation will start to change the way you feel about it, causing your feelings of stress to be reduced.

Thought Attacks™ are only harmful for as long as they stay in your mind.

Putting the Red Card into practise.

Take a moment to think about a challenging situation that is causing you to feel stressed right now.

Step 1 | **Recognise that your Thought Attacks™ are harming you.**

The situation is not the cause of your stress, it's your negative interpretation of it that is causing you to feel tense. This pressure is not good for you.

Step 2 | **Acknowledge that you have the power to choose different thoughts.**

No one is forcing you to think in this particular way; you have the power to choose different thoughts about the situation. You are not a victim to your situation or thoughts. You are the master of your mind.

Step 3 | **Ask yourself: How else can I interpret this situation?**

Start to think about the situation in another way. Search for a new meaning in this challenging circumstance. Think about the positive aspects that may arise from it. Think about what opportunities can come about because of it.

Now, keep your mind focused on your new interpretation. Fill your mind with a new possibility of how this threatening or unpleasant situation can lead to a positive outcome.

Remember that deeply embedded in every challenging situation is a precious gift. This gift is often hard to find as it's covered in negativity, pessimism and gloom. At first you may think that there is no benefit doing this in the midst of an extremely stressful situation. However, when you dig a little deeper and are ready to find the courage to get out of your comfort zone (or discomfort zone) you'll start to see things differently.

Imagine how you would feel if you believed that in every difficult situation there was a reward hidden, just waiting to be found? Life would have new meaning and what you once viewed as a stressful situation would be transformed into a worthwhile experience.

Summarising Resilience Builder 1:
Transforming your Thought Attacks™

1 The way we think usually determines the way we feel.

2 When we think negative thoughts we experience Thought Attacks™.

3 Thought Attacks™ are harmful and make you feel stressed.

4 Every challenge contains a gift especially for you. Your mission is to find it.

5 Making a commitment to use the Red Card technique when you're feeling stressed will transform your thinking.

Resilience Builder 2:
Asking the right questions

When experiencing a stressful event we often start to ask silent questions in our minds, without even being aware of it.

For example, when thinking about a stressful situation you may ask yourself:

Why is life always so difficult?   *What have I done to deserve this?*
What was I thinking?   *Why is this happening to me?*

These types of questions are what I call poor quality questioning because they affirm you as a victim of your circumstances and produce feelings of stress. They also don't make you feel any better about your situation.

When you ask yourself the question: *Why is life always so difficult?* you're setting yourself up for a pessimistic outlook by reaffirming that life is difficult and that you are powerless against its hardships. Is life really difficult all the time or would it be more accurate to say that sometimes we face challenges that need to be overcome and are part of the journey of our lives?

It's important to be constantly aware of the questions you are asking yourself because poor quality questions often create feelings of stress and prevent you from being optimistic by focusing your thoughts on all the negative aspects of your situation. These thoughts often snowball and, before you know it, you become stressed and anxious. By checking your inner questioning and ensuring that you're asking constructive questions your feelings of stress will be kept at bay.

So how do you turn poor quality questions into constructive ones?

The first step is to become aware of your poor quality questions and to make a conscious effort to be mindful of your inner chatter. Observe your self-talk closely and keep continual watch over it.

The next step is to become aware of the harmful nature of poor quality questions and the stress they can create. When you are mindful of the questions you are asking yourself, you'll be able to identify if they are of poor quality and how to replace them with constructive questions.

Here are a few constructive questions to consider:
- What can I learn from this experience?
- How can I use this situation to learn more about myself?
- Where is the opportunity in this problem?
- How can I ensure that I don't repeat the situation?
- How can I use this experience to learn patience and tolerance?
- How could I have prevented this problem?
- What can I do differently next time?

By consciously asking yourself questions like these you reframe a potentially stressful situation into one that can be a valuable experience for you.

Putting it into practise

Start by becoming aware of your inner questioning throughout the day. Focus your awareness on what questions you're asking yourself silently in your mind; it's this inner chatter that you need to become more familiar with.

Once you are aware of your inner questioning it will be easier to recognise poor quality questions when they arise.

Let's use a practical example to see how we can change poor quality questioning in a stressful situation.

You've been asked to report on an important project that you've been responsible for in a weekly work meeting. Unfortunately, things have not gone according to plan and you need to tell everyone why the project is no longer on track.

Response 1:
Poor quality questioning
(Usual default thinking)

While you're waiting to deliver your report your mind starts to stream poor quality questions.

You start asking yourself:

What are they going to think of me?

What if they take me off this project?

How will I ever get that bonus I want?

You start feeling stressed and anxious.

Response 2:
Constructive questioning
(*D-Stress* way of thinking)

While you're waiting your mind starts asking quality questions.

You ask yourself:

How can I use this situation to my advantage?

What lessons have I learned from this experience?

What if I focus on showing them my problem solving abilities and the benefits that this challenging situation has brought about?

You start to see a solution to your stressful situation and begin to relax.

Asking constructive questions helps you manage stress in challenging circumstances and maintain a positive state of mind.

Get to know the content of your inner chatter and be mindful of any negative questioning that may sabotage your feelings of optimism.

If you find that your questioning is creating a pessimistic view of a situation, change your focus by asking yourself constructive questions. You'll become open to a way of thinking that supports you in life's challenges.

Asking constructive questions helps you manage stress in challenging circumstances.

Summarising Resilience Builder 2:
Asking the right questions

1. The quality of the questions we ask ourselves in a stressful situation impact the way we feel about it.

2. Poor quality questions are those that create a pessimistic view of a situation and cause feelings of stress.

3. Listening to and monitoring your inner chatter will enable you to identify poor quality questioning and change it.

4. Choosing constructive questions enables you to manage and reduce stress.

5. Practise asking yourself constructive questions when experiencing a stressful situation.

$\{45$

Resilience Builder 3:
Focusing on the now

The mind is such a powerful tool; it determines the way you see the world. Your current view of yourself and your life is formed by the way your mind thinks about them and, in doing so, creates your reality. It also does something else that can cause feelings of stress. It projects thoughts into the future and can paint a negative picture about the way a situation can unfold. This is called negative mind projection.

The mind often does this when it's concerned about a particular situation that has yet to occur. It tries to gain control of this future situation by hypothesising various outcomes of the way it believes it may play out.

Here's an example:
Imagine you have been asked to make a short presentation at your end of year staff party. This is a function that everyone in the company attends and something people look forward to. It's also a wonderful opportunity to get to know the senior executives in a more casual manner.

Later on you start to think about your presentation. Your mind starts to churn out countless thoughts about it. You start to second guess your ability to present in front of everyone and start to think about what would happen if it didn't go well. Before you know it you've played out the whole evening in your mind and breakout in a cold sweat just thinking about all the potentially disastrous scenarios that could occur.

This negative mind projection is what often causes feelings of stress and anxiety. When you perceive a future event to be potentially threatening or unpleasant, you allow stress the opportunity to enter your body.

So why do we negative mind project in the first place?

What benefit does it give us?

The answer is interesting. The ego, which takes responsibility for our feelings of adequacy and worth, makes a promise. It promises that it will look after our self-esteem and protect us from anything that may compromise it. It does so by creating the feeling that we are in control of our lives. As a result, it prepares us for what could happen in the future by presenting the worst case scenario for any future events. What better way to protect the ego than by pointing out all the potentially threatening or embarrassing possibilities?

This is how the ego tricks us, by creating the illusion that it will protect and prepare us for these future scenarios. The reality is that all it offers is a vague hypothesis of what may or may not happen.

Negative mind projection creates feelings of stress when you feel the pain of a future event going wrong as if it is actually happening to you in the present. You live your future experience as if it was fast tracked into your present moment. This is the ego's attempt to bring some kind of control to an unknown event in the future.

The consequence of negative mind projection is that it destroys the quality of the present moment and replaces it with anxiety and stress.

So what can you do to stop your mind from projecting in this way?

As we've already learnt, if you leave your mind alone without a particular focus it will often default to thinking negatively. In order for you to master your mind and control your feelings of stress you need to instruct it otherwise. If you let it default you take the risk of allowing these thoughts to control you.

In mastering your mind you need to tell it how you want it to serve you. It can't be your servant if you allow it to use negative mind projection. Remember, you don't have a crystal ball to see into the future and it's not possible to know for certain how every future situation will unfold. Don't waste your thoughts trying to predict the unknown. Time is better spent setting goals, desires and intentions rather than worrying about whether they'll actually happen.

As soon as you become aware that you are feeling stressed about future situations, use your mind to focus your thoughts on how you would like the situation to turn out. Think about it optimistically and bring your attention back to your actions in the present moment. Inevitably, your mind will keep projecting your thoughts into the future so keep them focused on a positive outcome.

Be mindful that the only thing that is real is the present moment. The past is history and the future is unknown. When your focus is maintained on your present actions the feeling of stress will minimise.

Be mindful that the only thing that is real is the present moment.

How much stress are you feeling right now as you are reading these words?

Often we don't feel stress when fully immersed in an activity. It's only when we disengage from an activity and think negatively about something in the past or future that feelings of stress can arise.

The power of present moment focus comes about when you appreciate that it is the culmination of all your present actions that create your future. By focusing your attention on your actions in the present and thinking about your future as a product of these actions, you'll worry less about controlling it. If you find that your thoughts keep wondering about the future, focus them on the appropriate actions that can create the future you desire.

Once you gain confidence that your present moment actions will progress you further to your desired future, you'll feel better knowing that you are getting closer to your goals.

Be mindful of not making your future destinations more important than your actions in the present moment. If you do, you'll have high expectations and may be disappointed if they don't work out. Set goals and intentions for the future but don't become attached to their fulfilment by thinking incessantly about them.

When you keep your eyes on your future you have no eyes on the present. And when you have no eyes on the present you cannot work towards the future you want.

> When you have no eyes on the present you cannot work towards the future you want.

It's also useful to appreciate that sometimes results don't show up at the time you expect them to. This doesn't mean that you're on the wrong track.

Actions take time to germinate so be patient and make sure you don't start to over-dramatise an unsuccessful outcome unnecessarily.

Summarising Resilience Builder 3:
Focusing on the now

1 Stress can occur when we start to think negatively about a future outcome. This is called negative mind projection.

2 When we think about the future outcome of an event we often use negative mind projection to protect the ego.

3 When you find yourself negatively mind projecting, bring your focus back to your actions in the present.

4 Be mindful not to make your future destinations more important than the present actions that will help get you there.

5 You will not gain control of your future by hypothesising about it.

{51

Resilience Builder 4:
Telling a different story

Often we are unaware that the majority of our communication consists of telling stories about the experiences we've had. We do this because we want to share information, seek advice or get confirmation about the actions we've taken.

Think about the last conversation you had with a friend. What did you speak about? What experience did you relate to that person? What story did you tell?

Allow me to share the experience of a very special woman.

Many years ago one of my coaching clients asked if she could come and see me about a personal problem that had kept her on medication for depression and in therapy for 4 years. She told me that she could not find a meaningful relationship which she wanted so badly.

Her life dream was to get married and to be a loving mother. She felt that this dream would never be realised because of the many scars on her body from the numerous operations she had had as a child. A defect was found at birth and life saving procedures left the skin on her body disfigured.

The story she had been telling herself and others was that no man would ever find her attractive and that her body was an embarrassment to herself, and anybody else who might see it.

She had been telling that story for over 10 years and it made her feel ugly and despondent. The stress of thinking that she would be alone for the rest of her life started to take its toll and she found herself in a severe state of depression. This resulted in her losing many friends and being demoted to a less stressful position within her company.

After many months of discussions together she finally realised how the story she had been telling herself (and others) for so many years precluded her from finding the relationship she wanted and deserved.

She also understood that it was only a story and that by creating another she could make herself feel a lot better. So she decided to change her story.

Now she tells it like this:

The scars on my body are the result of the life saving procedures I had as a child. I courageously fought to stay alive and I won! They are my memories to appreciate the gift of life. They serve as a reminder to not take my life for granted and to have a reverence for the beauty of life. Most of us need constant reminders of this and I have it right on tap.

After repeating this new story silently to herself every day for a month things started to change for her. She no longer felt embarrassed about her body and started to love herself, seeing being alive as a gift. Her depression began to lift and she opened the door to seeing her own worth and beauty. Our sessions ended and I asked her to keep in touch.

About eighteen months later I received a very excited call from her telling me that she had met a lovely, kind and gentle man and that they had decided to get married. She also got her old job back.

This is just an example of a story one person created, a story in which they cast themselves as the hero and not the victim.

What are the stories you have been repeating to yourself that are holding you back from realising your dreams or keeping your old wounds from healing? What stories are you telling about your abilities, relationships, health, finances, friends or circumstances? Without even being aware of it you may be repeating certain stories and beliefs over and over until it is so deeply embedded within you that it becomes your truth. It can become so ingrained that any distortion you may create along the way is accepted by you as the truth, so long as you repeat it often enough.

> Without even being aware of it you may be repeating certain stories and beliefs over and over until it is so deeply embedded within you that it becomes your truth.

I know this because of the story I used to tell.

When I migrated to Australia I decided to start my own training and coaching business. I thought it would take about 9 months to a year to get it up and running. Unfortunately things didn't go as planned as I was unaware of all the complexities of starting a business in a new country with a completely different business culture. After about 18 months I still had not progressed very far and started to tell myself and others how difficult it was to break into the market. I told a story that painted a picture of an arduous and problematic process that made me feel unhappy and stressed.

After repeating it to many people, many times, I started to believe that it would be a long, hard road to success. When others heard my story they agreed that it was tough to start a business with so much competition, especially when I didn't have a network of people that could help me build my business. They gave me more negative information which I built into my (already) miserable story.

One morning, when I was jogging on the beach, I recognised that these thoughts weren't helping me and realised that I had been telling a pessimistic and gloomy story about something I really wanted. How could it ever happen when this was the way I believed it would turn out? No wonder I was feeling stressed and my business wasn't booming!

I had caught myself telling a story that I knew would not help me succeed. I told it because I wanted empathy and confirmation that I was not a failure. I wanted others to affirm that my lack of success was the result of my challenging situation and that I was not to blame. I chose to be the victim.

If I was to change my situation I needed to tell a different story; I knew I had to turn my thinking around. I thought about it for a while and decided to change my story and tell it like this:

It's normal for a new business to take time to get off the ground and flourish. I am making the right choices and taking the right actions. Success is just around the corner. I believe that what I have to offer is of value and will be well-received.

Six weeks later I got my first contract.

So often we repeat stories in which we play the victim until eventually we believe that there isn't much we can do about a situation and our fate is sealed. As victims it's difficult to see an optimistic view of a situation and we feel disempowered, creating fertile ground for stress to flourish.

Here's an example of how we use storytelling in our everyday lives and cast ourselves as victims or heroes.

Peter is a person that always seems to be complaining about how stressful his work is and how little time he has to spend with his family. At every opportunity Peter talks about how stressed he feels to friends and associates. What's interesting is that the people he talks to empathise with him. They feel the same way, appreciate his plight and commiserate with his unfortunate situation.

Every time Peter tells his story he confirms himself as a victim to his circumstances and perpetuates his feelings of stress. After a while people start to identify him with his story. As soon as they see him they think: Here comes poor, stressed Peter that works crazy hours!

Furthermore, Peter may start to feel that he always needs to appear stressed in order for his story to be believed and for it to gain credibility.

By repeating his story over and over his condition never changes and his cycle of stress continues. So how does Peter start to change a story he's been repeating for many years? The challenge he faces is that he has become used to talking about why things won't change rather than how things can change. He's stuck in a rut of negative self-talk and has become used to talking about himself as a victim.

What is important for Peter to know is that he has the power to choose how he would like to interpret what is happening in his life. He may be experiencing something extremely challenging but that doesn't mean he has to speak about it in a negative way, which will almost certainly make him feel worse.

Putting it into practise

Now it's your turn.

What story are you telling? Are you choosing to tell a story that casts you as the victim, potentially causing you to feel stressed? Remember that you're in charge of the story's content and how it unfolds. You can choose to triumph or be the victim.

To ensure you are the former, be mindful of what you say and how you say it. Be aware when you start talking about the negative aspects of yourself or a situation. Recognise that your negative story will cause feelings of stress.

To reduce stressful feelings you need to change the things you say and the stories you relate. Start practising by talking about the positive aspects of an experience rather than focusing on what went wrong. Sometimes you may feel overwhelmed by the threat or pain that a situation may cause and find it difficult to relate your experience in a positive light. However, if you cultivate a positive attitude to your challenging circumstances you will start to see problems and difficulties as opportunities with a benefit, rather than situations that simply cause you stress.

Everything can teach you something about yourself, someone else or life in general, if you allow it to do so. Opportunities

> You're in charge of the story's content and how it unfolds.

and benefits are often hidden in what we see as problems. When you view a stressful situation as a window of opportunity you begin to realise that it's not a situation that determines feelings of stress but rather the way you perceive it and relate your story.

Does Nelson Mandela talk about his pain and suffering, asking for sympathy and comfort? Or does he talk about how he rose above it and how he would not allow his horrific situation to bring him down? While we may not all be as advanced as Mr. Mandela we are blessed with the ability to choose our responses and attitudes to the situations we face.

Talk about how you can turn a potentially negative situation into one that can be of benefit to you. Talk about what you have learned through a particularly painful or stressful experience. It may feel a little strange when you first start talking about the positive aspects of a stressful situation. You might be so accustomed to talking about the negative aspects that you may feel you're not being genuine or authentic when you relate stressful situations in a positive light. Don't let that be of concern to you, just keep your focus.

Remember how uncomfortable it was when you had your first driving lesson and how now you find yourself driving home almost automatically and don't even remember the trip? Soon thinking positively will come to you just as naturally.

Commit to talking about your experiences in a positive way.

Ask your colleagues, friends and family to point out to you whenever you are playing the role of the victim in your stories. Make a habit of sharing good news. With practise and mindfulness it will soon become second nature so commit to talking about your experiences in a positive way.

Summarising Resilience Builder 4:
Telling a different story

1. Most of our communication consists of relating stories about our experiences.

2. Become aware of the way you tell your stories to others.

3. If you paint a bleak picture of a situation the possibility of feeling stressed increases.

4. Commit to relating stories that have positive outcomes.

5. Make a habit of telling people the positive aspects of a stressful situation.

{61

Resilience Builder 5:
Changing the labels

From a very young age we are taught to label our experiences as either good or bad. If a situation made us feel stressed we labelled it as bad. If it made us feel happy and cheerful we labelled it as good.

Labelling our experiences as either good or bad sets up a mind-set of polarity thinking. This means that we think in opposites: black and white; right and wrong; happy or sad; positive and negative. The problem with this kind of thinking is that it only gives us two choices in which to think about a situation. It's either one or the other. There is no grey and because we so often default to thinking negatively the chances are we will, more often than not, choose the bad label.

Take the following example that I experienced back in 1989.

I was in my final year at university and had failed one subject in my Bachelor of Commerce degree by 3 percentage points. I pleaded with the examiners to mark my exam again in the hope of finding those 3 precious points. They agreed but there were no extra marks to be found. The grade stood as it was and I had to repeat the year.

At the time conscription was compulsory in South Africa and I had planned to start my 2 years of military service with my friends the following year. Now I was to stay on at university while they were completing their first year. They would be half way through their training when I was due to start! I was in disbelief and so upset and angry with myself. This was a bad situation and I was miserable.

The year began and, seeing that I only had one subject to complete, I had lots of free time. I loved music and decided to start a band and teach guitar from home in my spare time. The year went by in a flash and I had a fun, carefree year. Thankfully, I managed to pass my exam this time.

Although my friends had had a tough year, they were happy they only had one to go. Now it was my turn to start two years of gruelling military training.

The new year was fast approaching and I was preparing for what I dreaded the most. Two years of military service, alone and without my friends by my side to support me. I lamented on how bad my situation was and that I would be enrolled in the army grouped with total strangers under harsh conditions.

Three weeks before I was to report for duty, I woke up to a big news story taking the media by storm. Conscription was being phased out and the government was committed to taking immediate action. From the next intake any person enrolling in the military would only need to complete one year of compulsory service.

I was ecstatic! I would only have to endure one year of service. Had I passed my exam I would have been slogging it out with my friends in the army. Instead, I had had one of the best years of my life and, to top it all off, I would finish my military service at the same time as them.

The point of sharing this story is that we never really know when something is a good thing or a bad thing. Can you know for certain which of your experiences will be good or bad upfront? How often have you labelled an experience as bad and it turned out to be favourable in the end?

We rarely know how things will turn out and by preemptively labelling something we take the risk of either becoming stressed for no reason or being disappointed down the track.

When you label something as bad, your focus and attention is directed to all the negative aspects of the situation and your outlook becomes bleak. The same goes for your emotions and the creation of stress. The irony of labelling something as bad is that you may cause the outcome of the situation to be negative by focusing your attention on creating that scenario. If you take a more unbiased view of your situation by refusing to label it you become objective and reduce the possibility of creating unnecessary stress.

To do this you need to change the labels you give your experiences. Stay away from labelling things as good or bad and try using different terminology, such as interesting, unique challenging, exciting, different, transforming, etc.

> **If you take a more unbiased view of your situation by refusing to label it you become objective and reduce the possibility of creating unnecessary stress.**

Putting it into practise

Take a moment to think about a situation you're in right now that is causing you to feel stressed.

| Step 1 | Check to see if you have placed any labels on it. Are you calling the situation bad, stressful, hopeless, irritating, depressing, frustrating, etc? |

| Step 2 | Once you have identified the label recognise that it is responsible for the way you are feeling. |

| Step 3 | Change the label. Think of terminology you can use to describe the situation in a more positive way. Choose the label that best describes the way you would like to feel about the situation. |

| Step 4 | Talk about the situation using the new label. |

| Step 5 | Check your levels of stress. |

Living each day as an opportunity to develop an understanding of yourself and others makes life an exciting adventure. With this mind-set the notion of a bad experience ceases to exit, instead becoming something that paves the way for growth and opportunity.

> Living each day as an opportunity to develop an understanding of yourself and others makes life an exciting adventure.

Summarising Resilience Builder 5:
Changing the labels

1. Labelling your experience impacts the way you feel about it.

2. Stress is created by labelling situations in a negative way.

3. Avoid labelling a situation as either good or bad.

4. If you have used a negative label change it by viewing the situation more positively.

5. Choose a label that best describes the way you would like to feel about a situation.

{67

Resilience Builder 6:
Observing the feeling

When we talk about being stressed we're really talking about a feeling. We don't think stress, we feel stress. The only way you know that you're experiencing stress is through your senses. The feeling of stress resides somewhere inside your body and it's your body that sends you signals that the feeling of stress is present.

Everyone experiences stress differently. Some feel it in their chest area, their stomachs or in their solar plexus. Others may feel it in their head, neck or shoulders. It's important for you to recognise that stress does not live anywhere but inside of you, residing in a specific place in your body.

To reduce and manage your stress you need to have a relationship with it. This can only be done if you are able to access your stress and find the place in your body where you feel it. Once you've identified where it lives you can manage and reduce the stressful feeling by observing it.

So how does a stressful feeling subside just by watching it? It works like this. The stress you experience is not caused by the situation but by the thoughts you have about it. When you observe the feeling and become totally present with it you let go of the thoughts that created it. The feeling starts to

> It's important for you to recognise that stress does not live anywhere but inside of you, residing in a specific place in your body.

subside as it no longer has any fuel to keep it alive. As long as you keep your focus on the feeling, and not on your worrying thoughts, the stress will start to dissipate.

For example, a person who feels stress as tightness in the chest area knows that when he experiences that tightness stress has arisen in his body. His body has given him the physical signals that stress is present.

When I was 32 years old I decided to finally overcome the fear of drowning that had plagued me since childhood. I took the brave step and enrolled in a scuba diving course. The procedure was that we practised the techniques in the pool before attempting it in the ocean.

I was a little nervous during the pool exercises but when I was about to backflip off the dive boat and go down 8 meters into the ocean, I became terrified!

I sat at the edge of the boat and felt my heart pounding against my chest. My breathing turned from normal to hyperventilation within a few seconds and my palms started to sweat. I was in a severe state of panic. The fear that I was trying to overcome was taking over my body and I started to think my worst nightmare was about to come true.

I knew that I couldn't dive under these conditions and that if I did, I ran the risk of something going horribly wrong. I asked the instructor for more time; I needed to find a way to control my stress and I needed to do it quickly.

I closed my eyes and started to focus on my heart that felt as though it was beating out of control. It was racing and thumping so intensely that I could almost hear it. I had to get my body into a calmer state. I decided to stop and really feel the feeling, observing the sensations in my heart and nothing else. I felt it pushing up against my chest with every beat. I observed my chest expanding and contracting and felt the force of air through my nostrils with every breath. I didn't try to change my breathing in any way or make it slow down; I just observed it without judgement.

Fearful thoughts started to enter my mind but I knew that I needed to let them go and not allow any distractions to take me away from being present with the feeling. After a few minutes I felt the pounding in my heart alter its pace and start to slow. The sensation in my heart was changing and I could feel it slow, gradually losing intensity.

A few minutes passed and I started to feel more at ease. My feelings of terror were replaced with feelings of nervousness and apprehension. These feelings weren't debilitating and I knew that I was ready to finally conquer my fear.

I backflipped off the boat and overcame my fear. It was one of the most memorable experiences of my life.

Putting it into practise

Now take some time to contemplate where your stress manifests itself in your body.

Think about a situation which is currently causing you stress. Where do you feel the sensation when you're stressed? What does it feel like? How intense does it get? How long does it last?

Step 1 | Identify the area in your body where your stress manifests itself. Do you feel it in your chest or stomach? Does it manifest itself as pain in your neck or back? Feel where the stress is situated in your body.

Step 2 | Put all your attention on that area and just observe the sensation. Don't try to analyse it or think about the situation that caused it, just focus on the sensation. If it becomes more intense just observe its intensity. If it moves somewhere else in your body, observe its movement. Don't try to force any change in it or try to make it go away, just accept the feeling.

Observe it like you're watching a movie. What kind of sensation is it? Is it a sharp or pulsating feeling? Does it cause pain? What kind of pain is it? Try to really enter the sensation.

If you walked into a room and it was filled with this sensation, what would the room feel like? What is the temperature inside the room? Does the sensation have a colour associated with it? How would you describe it? What words come to mind when you feel the sensation?

Get to know the feeling well and just be with it without trying to change it.

You may find that when you're observing the feeling your mind begins to wonder and starts to think about the stressful situation again. When that happens (and chances are it will happen) simply bring back your focus to the sensation inside your body. You may need to do this many times so don't become disheartened or frustrated. The more you practise the easier it will become.

Step 3 | Observe the sensation until it starts to subside and is reduced to a level that is manageable for you.

This technique requires you only to remain focused on the sensations in your body and when you do you'll notice that your feelings of stress will be reduced. They may not disappear but the important thing is to get them to a level that is manageable for you. Be patient and the rewards will pay off.

The mind is so used to being left alone without instruction that it often defaults to thinking negatively and perpetuates your feelings of stress. Observing your feelings will enable you to start controlling your mind by giving it something to focus on rather than letting it run on its own. This does require practise but in time you will eventually train your mind to serve you.

Summarising Resilience Builder 6:
Observing the feeling

1. Stress manifests itself as a sensation in our bodies.

2. To manage and reduce stress you need to know exactly where the stress is in your body.

3. We can access stress by identifying the sensation that it creates our bodies.

4. Focusing on the physical sensation will reduce the feeling of stress.

5. It's not about erasing the stress completely; it's about reducing it to a level that's manageable.

Resilience Builder 7:
Developing a sense of gratitude

You may be wondering how developing a sense of gratitude can help you manage your stress better.

When you think about how lucky you are to have the things you have and feel thankful, you stop stressing about the things you don't have.

Stress is often caused from feelings of deficiency. If you believe that you don't have or won't have enough of something stressful feelings can arise. When your thoughts become focused on what is lacking it's difficult to sponsor positive emotions. By thinking thoughts of gratitude and abundance in challenging situations you can keep your stressful thoughts at bay.

By thinking thoughts of gratitude and abundance in challenging situations you can keep your stressful thoughts at bay.

Let's use a practical example to explain this:

John has been stressed about being unemployed. For the past 5 weeks he has attended many interviews but is yet to find the right job. His mind begins to think incessantly about not being able to find the job he wants and he starts to feel stressed and anxious. He starts to think that his skills are outdated, that he's not good enough to get a job or that he'll never find a job again.

Let's analyse John's thoughts:
Some of his thoughts are the facts about the situation **(factual thoughts)** while others are thoughts created from lack and insufficiency **(scarcity thoughts)**.

> When he says to himself:
> *I have been to so many interviews and still nothing has proved to be suitable.*
> **(This is factual thinking)**
>
> *What if there are no jobs available?*
> **(This is scarcity thinking)**
>
> *What if I can't afford to pay my mortgage?*
> **(This is scarcity thinking)**

If John's thoughts continue along these lines it's likely that he will start to feel stressed when he thinks about all the potentially disastrous outcomes that could occur. He may even start to experience high levels of anxiety and disturbed sleep. Scarcity thinking has resulted in John feeling stressed.

What if John factored in the feeling of gratitude and abundance in his thinking?

He might start to think:
Nothing has come about yet.

(This is factual thinking)

I feel appreciative that I have never been unemployed before.
(This is gratitude thinking)

I know it's just a matter of time until the right job comes along.
(This is abundant thinking)

By thinking in this way John can reduce his feelings of stress because he's focusing his thoughts on gratitude and abundance rather than on feelings of scarcity.

Next time you're feeling stressed, think about all the things that you're grateful for in your particular situation. It's important that whenever you're stressed you counter the feeling by thinking thoughts of gratitude, appreciation, love, compassion and abundance. In doing so, your stress will begin to subside. Be mindful that as soon as you allow your mind to slip back to thoughts of scarcity your feelings of stress may return.

Remember that you always have a choice on how you want to feel. You can choose feelings of stress or feelings of gratitude and abundance. Make a commitment to be more grateful and appreciative of what you have everyday.

We all have many things to be grateful for. If you compare yourself to others that seem to have more than you, you will only increase your feelings of inadequacy and the potential for feeling stressed.

Put the stress in your life into perspective by appreciating the many things you are blessed to have.

Put the stress in your life into perspective by appreciating the many things you are blessed to have.

Putting it into practise

Think about your life for a moment.

What are you grateful for?

When you wake up in the morning do you feel pain in your body? Can you see? Can you walk? Do you have a roof over your head? Do you have food in your belly? Have you laughed today? Have you talked to a friend? Do have a job to go to? Do you have people that love and care for you?

You have a lot to be grateful for everyday, you just need to take the time to appreciate it.

By choosing the attitude of gratitude you are by no means negating or disregarding the challenges you experience. They are real and require your attention. However, by developing a sense of gratitude you will feel more appreciative and, consequently, less stressed.

Start to realise how lucky you are right now.

> **You have a lot to be grateful for everyday, you just need to take the time to appreciate it.**

Summarising Resilience Builder 7:
Developing a sense of gratitude

1. Focus your attention on everything you appreciate in your life.

2. Feel a sense of gratitude and appreciation whenever you can.

3. Be aware that thoughts of scarcity can create feelings of stress.

4. In a challenging situation you always have a choice to feel grateful or stressed. The choice is yours.

5. Put the stresses in your life into perspective and recognise that you have more to be grateful for than to feel stressed about.

section 04

A final word

It is my wish for you to be happy and live with peace of mind.

The universe is in constant abundance. Just look at how many stars there are in the sky, grains of sand on the earth, leaves on the trees, cells in our bodies, fish in the sea and the constant supply of the air we breathe.

Nature is a wonderful teacher of how we can manage stress. The autumn leaves just let go and fall off the branches with ease. Notice that the branch doesn't try to hang on to its leaves for fear that no other leaves will ever sprout again. It knows that new leaves will appear at the right time but only when the old ones fall off and give space for new life.

What do you need to let go of in order to create space for feelings of calm and peace? Old patterns and habits are hard to break but the reward for changing your thinking is growth, newness and a renewed excitement for life.

Stress stops you from letting go. It makes you smaller and turns your feelings of happiness and contentment into anxiety and apprehension. You can't love life if you choose to live with continuous feelings of stress. These feelings can ruin the quality of your life and limit your chances of living with ease and simplicity. It drains your life of the joy, lightness and excitement that each challenge potentially presents.

Imagine what life would be like without feeling burdened and victimised by life's seemingly threatening intentions.

Imagine being in love with life.

Imagine feeling a deep sense of gratitude for living on this earth and being thankful that you can enjoy the wonder of what each new day might bring.

We all know that life presents its fair share of challenges. We all know that terrible things can happen and that life is not always easy. For this reason it's even more essential to embrace the things that go well in your life and celebrate them.

Make an agreement with yourself to find something you're grateful for everyday. Tap into that feeling and enjoy it. Feel what it's like to have a heightened sense of gratitude and thankfulness. When gratitude becomes the lens through which you view the world you'll take a different perspective when things don't go so well.

Make another commitment to yourself. Choose at least one of the techniques I have shared with you in this book and practise it for 21 days, in succession. After 21 days it will become a habit and it will form your new way of thinking. This is the *D-Stress* way of thinking.

Treat each technique with the respect and reverence it deserves. They come from wise and humble people that have walked similar paths to us and have found the way to live a contented and peaceful life.

This fresh and liberating way of thinking will be your best friend, supporting you every time stress comes knocking on your door. It will enable you to cope with what life throws at you and give you the armour and protection you need to overcome life's challenges.

You may be wondering if I live a completely stress free life, being well versed in these 7 techniques. Of course I don't. I have drifted off the path many times and continue to feel stress on occasion.

What gets me back on track is that I don't allow any of my Thought Attacks™ to stay for longer than a few seconds. It has been the practise and perseverance of these techniques that has enabled me to limit the danger that stress can create in my life. I have learnt to control it because I carry the tools with me, in my mind, everyday.

Now that you have come to the end of the book you're probably telling yourself you'll start practising the techniques tomorrow, next week or next month. Next time you have a free moment.

Let me tell you a secret.

There will never be a right time and there will always be distractions.

Just start now.

The reward of feeling composed, peaceful and self-assured in the midst of turmoil far outweighs the discipline required to integrate these techniques into your life. Make time for them. Your happiness depends on it.

Now is the perfect time to start.

Right now.

So take a deep breath and get ready for the ride.

Quick reference: D-Stress Resilience Builders

Resilience builder 1:
Transforming your Thought Attacks™

1. The way we think usually determines the way we feel.

2. When we think negative thoughts we experience Thought Attacks™.

3. Thought Attacks™ are harmful and make you feel stressed.

4. Every challenge contains a gift especially for you. Your mission is to find it.

5. Making a commitment to use the Red Card technique when you're feeling stressed will transform your thinking.

Resilience Builder 2:
Asking the right questions

1. The quality of the questions we ask ourselves in a stressful situation impact the way we feel about it.

2. Poor quality questions are those that create a pessimistic view of a situation and cause feelings of stress.

3. Listening to and monitoring your inner-chatter will enable you to identify poor quality questioning and change it.

4. Choosing constructive questions enables you to manage and reduce stress.

5. Practise asking yourself constructive questions when experiencing a stressful situation.

Resilience Builder 3:
Focusing on the now

1. Stress can occur when we start to think negatively about a future outcome. This is called negative mind projection.

2. When we think about the future outcome of an event we often use negative mind projection to protect the ego.

3. When you find yourself negatively mind projecting, bring your focus back to your actions in the present.

4. Be mindful not to make your future destinations more important than the present actions that will help get you there.

5. You will not gain control of your future by hypothesising about it.

Resilience Builder 4:
Telling a different story

1. Most of our communication consists of relating stories about our experiences.

2. Become aware of the way you tell your stories to others.

3. If you paint a bleak picture of a situation the possibility of feeling stressed increases.

4. Commit to relating stories that have positive outcomes.

5. Make a habit of telling people the positive aspects of a stressful situation.

Resilience Builder 5:
Changing the labels

1. Labelling your experience impacts the way you feel about it.
2. Stress is created by labelling situations in a negative way.
3. Avoid labelling a situation as either good or bad.
4. If you have used a negative label change it by viewing the situation more positively.
5. Choose a label that best describes the way you would like to feel about a situation.

Resilience Builder 6:
Observing the feeling

1. Stress manifests itself as a sensation in our bodies.
2. To manage and reduce stress you need to know exactly where the stress is in your body.
3. We can access stress by identifying the sensation that it creates our bodies.
4. Focusing on the physical sensation will reduce the feeling of stress.
5. It's not about erasing the stress completely; it's about reducing it to a level that's manageable.

Resilience Builder 7:
Developing a sense of gratitude

1. Focus your attention on everything you appreciate in your life.

2. Feel a sense of gratitude and appreciation whenever you can.

3. Be aware that thoughts of scarcity can create feelings of stress.

4. In a challenging situation you always have a choice to feel grateful or stressed. The choice is yours.

5. Put the stresses in your life into perspective and recognise that you have more to be grateful for than to feel stressed about.

Bibliography

Albrecht, Karl, *Brain Power: Learn to Improve Your Thinking Skills,*
USA: Fireside, 1980.

Branham, Leigh, *The 7 Hidden Reasons Employees Leave: How to Recognise the Subtle Signs and Act Before it's Too Late,*
New York: AMACOM, 2005.

Brewin, Chris, *Cognitive Foundations of Clinical Psychology,*
USA: Psychology Press, 1988.

Browne, Neil and Kelley, Stuart M., *Asking the Right Questions: A Guide to Critical Thinking,*
USA: Prentice Hall, 2006.

Byron, Katie and Mitchell, Stephen, *Loving What Is: Four Questions that Can Change Your Life,*
USA: Three Rivers Press, 2003.

Chopra, Deepak, Peace is the Way: Bringing War and Violence to an End,
USA: Three Rivers Press, 2005

Chopra, Deepak, Quantum Healing: Exploring the Frontiers of
Mind/Body Medicine,
USA: Bantam, 1990.

Hill, Napoleon and Stone, W., *Success Through a Positive Mental Attitude,*
USA: Pocket Books, 2007.

Maltz, Maxwell, *Psycho-Cybernetics,*
USA: Prentice Hall Press, 2002.

Millman, Dan, *Way of the Peaceful Warrior,*
USA: HJ Kramer, 2006.

O'Donohue, William, Fisher, Jane E. and Hayes, Steven C.,
Cognitive Behavior Therapy: Applying Empirically Supported Techniques in Your Practice,
USA: Wiley, 2003.

Porter, Kay, *The Mental Athlete: Inner Training for Peak Performance in All Sports,*
USA: Human Kinetics Publishers, 2003.

Riesbeck, Christopher K. and Schank, Roger C.,
Inside Case-Based Reasoning,
USA: Lawrence Erlbaum, 1989.

Sarma, Kamal, *Mental Resilience: The Power of Clarity: How to Develop the Focus of a Warrior and the Peace of a Monk,*
USA: New World Library, 2008.

Song, Cai and Leonard, Brian E., *Fundamentals of Psychoneuroimmunology,*
USA: Wiley, 2000.

Stevens, Tom G., You Can Choose to be Happy: Rise Above Anxiety, Anger and Depression,
USA: Wheeler Sutton Publishing Company, 1998.

Tolle, Eckhart, *The Power of Now: A Guide to Spiritual Enlightenment,* USA: New World Library, 2004.

Tolle, Eckhart, *Practicing the Power of Now: Essential Teachings, Meditations and Exercises from The Power of Now,*
USA: New World Library, 2001.

Wright, Jesse H., Ramirez Basco, Monica and Thase, Michael E., *Learning Cognitive-Behavior Therapy: An Illustrated Guide,*
USA: American Psychiatric Publishing, 2005.

section 05

Stress
health check

This informal stress health check will help you identify your current levels of stress and their causes.

Tick the boxes that apply to you and add the number of boxes ticked for each section. Total your scores for each section to find out which stress category you're in.

Workplace Stressors

Are you affected by any of the following work related stressors?

- ☐ Promotion or demotion
- ☐ Changes in pay
- ☐ Changes in working relationships
- ☐ Inadequate training
- ☐ Insufficient work breaks
- ☐ Excessive noise in workplace
- ☐ Bullying or harassment
- ☐ Restructuring, merger or acquisition
- ☐ Changes resulting in job insecurity
- ☐ Changes in workload
- ☐ Project deadlines
- ☐ Retirement
- ☐ Communication difficulties
- ☐ Cultural challenges
- ☐ Challenges in managing people
- ☐ Unresolved health and safety issues
- ☐ Change in working hours
- ☐ Starting a new job
- ☐ New management, team or boss
- ☐ Team management
- ☐ Managing workplace conflict

Number of boxes ticked ___

Physical Symptoms

Do you have any of the following physical symptoms?

- ☐ Headaches or migraines
- ☐ Depression
- ☐ Ulcers
- ☐ High blood pressure
- ☐ Anxiety
- ☐ Anger
- ☐ Insomnia or sleep disturbances
- ☐ Constant tiredness
- ☐ Lack of concentration
- ☐ Increased use of smoking, alcohol or drugs
- ☐ Heart palpitations
- ☐ Feeling fearful
- ☐ Skin rashes
- ☐ Forgetfulness
- ☐ Sweating
- ☐ Teeth grinding
- ☐ Nail biting

Number of boxes ticked ___

Personal Stressors

Are you currently affected by any of the following personal stressors?

- ☐ Weight issues
- ☐ Changes in financial status
- ☐ Work-life balance
- ☐ Spouse not working
- ☐ Low self-esteem
- ☐ Personal injury, illness or handicap
- ☐ End of a relationship or marriage
- ☐ Any substance abuse
- ☐ Death of family member or close friend
- ☐ Illness of family member
- ☐ Family member leaving home
- ☐ Family interpersonal issues
- ☐ Sexual concerns
- ☐ Personal health changes

Number of boxes ticked ___

Environmental Stressors

Are you currently affected by any of the following environmental stressors?

- ☐ Moving to a new country or city
- ☐ Experiencing a new culture
- ☐ Moving to a new house or apartment
- ☐ Cultural difficulties
- ☐ New climate
- ☐ Issues with crime
- ☐ Damage to property
- ☐ Loss of property
- ☐ Noise disturbances
- ☐ Pollution
- ☐ Changes in financial status of friends or family
- ☐ Neighbourhood changes
- ☐ Council issues
- ☐ Traffic or commuting issues
- ☐ Political changes
- ☐ Economic changes
- ☐ Managing technological advancements

Number of boxes ticked ___

TOTAL BOXES TICKED ___

Turn the page to learn about your current stress level.

Results

**If you scored 0–10:
Your stress level is low**

You seem to be handling your life situations constructively and have an ability to be resilient to the challenges you experience. Your confidence and self-esteem enable you to manage your stressful situations and you don't usually allow people or circumstances to get the better of you.

When you feel stressed you have the ability to get back on track quickly. If this score is low due to a particular occurrence e.g. You've just married, received a promotion or arrived back from a holiday, take a moment to reflect on whether you have the tools and techniques to cope if things change. Generally you are at ease and contented with your life and mostly feel positive and optimistic.

**If you scored 11–20:
Your stress level is normal**

Everyone has some degree of stress in their lives and although you may be experiencing some challenges, your stress is not at a level that you need to be concerned about. Turn the stress you feel into a positive in your life by seeing it as a motivator to reach the goals you are striving towards.

Overall you are satisfied with your current life situation, however there is some work to be done in managing your stress more effectively. Become familiar with the *D-Stress* resilience builders in this book as they will help you to better manage and reduce your stress when it arises. By practising these techniques you will start to feel calmer, contented and at ease.

**If you scored 21–30:
Your stress level is above average**

There are certain situations that are challenging for you and you may feel burdened by them and find it difficult to manage stress. Assess the main areas that are causing you to feel stressed and explore potential changes to those areas that are in your control.

Try as much as possible to minimise the minor stressors and not allow them to add additional pressure to your life. Start to focus on the way you would like your situation to be and work towards that goal. Ask your spouse, partner or a friend to help keep you on track and you won't feel alone in making those important changes.

Commit to practising the *D-Stress* resilience builders in this book as they will help you to reduce your stress levels and give you the tools to better manage any stressful situations in the future.

**If you scored 31 and above:
Your stress level is high**

It is likely that you are feeling overwhelmed and anxious. You may also be experiencing some physical problems as a result of stress so it's important for you to keep your health in check. Get help from someone you can depend on to overcome your stress and assist you in managing your situation.

There are solutions to your problems so make a commitment to change the situation you're in. It's not making you happy and it's up to you to make some changes even though they may be difficult to carry out. Ensure that you practise the *D-Stress* resilience builders in this book as they will help you cope more effectively with your stress. Remember that you have the choice to change the way you think about any situation.

Commit to thinking better about your life and start to focus on the way you want it to be. Be courageous, take action and things will get better.

Meiron Lees

Meiron's passion to understand human behaviour started when he was just 12 years old where he was often seen at the local library churning through books on psychology. He knew that this was his calling and that one day he would share this knowledge and help others.

After completing his Bachelor of Commerce Honors degree, Meiron became a director of a financial planning company in South Africa in 1991. Three years later he qualified to join the Million Dollar Round Table Association and in 1996, he formed a coaching and training division in the company.

Meiron is committed to the development of people through coaching and training programs in the areas of resilience, stress management and organisational development.

To date over 5000 leaders, managers, consultants and business owners have participated in his programs worldwide and he has won awards for his training excellence.

His clients include companies such as IBM, Citibank, Westpac, MTV Networks, PriceWaterhouseCoopers, Harvey World Travel and Symantec. He is a keynote speaker at conferences and events.

Meiron's approach is fresh, dynamic and unique. His user-friendly and practical techniques enable participants to implement strategies that create meaningful and positive change. He is committed to constant learning and improvement and ensures that his methodologies incorporate the latest research from both local and international sources.

His passion extends beyond the corporate arena and he has studied Reiki, becoming a Reiki Master in 1999. In his spare time he plays the guitar, piano and the African Djembe drum. He is also a keen cyclist, runner and scuba diver.

Author's Note

My intention for writing *D-Stress* is to help the many people around the world to manage and reduce the stress in their lives by building resilience. From my own experience, and the thousands of people that I have coached over the years, managing stress has been the greatest obstacle.

Through the journey of our lives we are often confronted with challenging situations that can derail our emotional contentment. However, we are not taught how to manage ourselves through times of resistance and our mental and physical health can be severely affected.

My wish for *D-Stress* is that it serves as a valuable and practical tool that will help lighten the weight that stress imposes and to empower it's readers that living with peace of mind and contentment is a real and tangible possibility.

Building resilience in challenging times

For Organisations

Book Meiron to speak at your next conference.

He has inspired audiences worldwide with his highly engaging and transformative keynote addresses.

Meiron also specialises in facilitating stress management and resilience programs.

He incorporates leading edge strategies and techniques in his programs and has trained over 5000 executives, managers and business owners both in Australia and internationally.

The following workshops have been instrumental in assisting executives, managers and employees to better manage stress and build resilience:

Topic 1: How to build a resilient culture

Topic 2: D-Stress techniques in the workplace

Topic 3: How to remain calm and in control in challenging situations

Topic 4: Top 10 workplace stress tips

Topic 5: Helping others to better manage stress

For Individuals

Meiron offers one-on-one D-Stress coaching specifically tailored to individual situations and requirements. Session options are telephonically, on Skype, Whatsapp or Viber and are held in the strictest confidence.

For more information on D-Stress programs please email Meiron at:

meiron@meironlees.com.au
or visit
www.meironlees.com.au/d-stress-coaching

3 STEP PROCESS
TO CONTROL YOUR

"thought attacks."™

meironlees

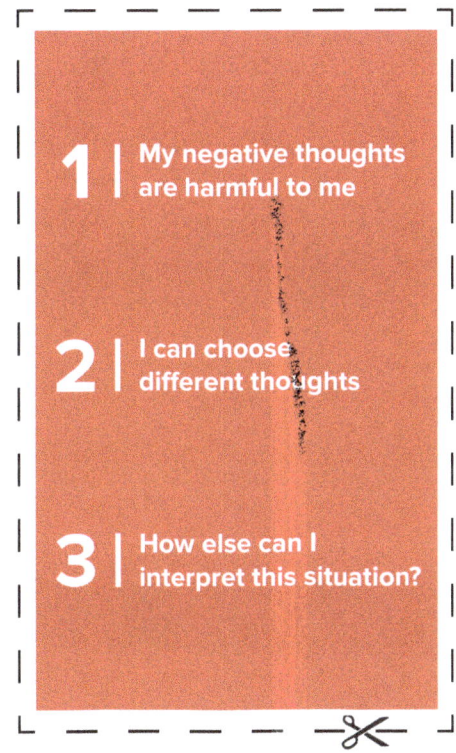

1 | My negative thoughts are harmful to me

2 | I can choose different thoughts

3 | How else can I interpret this situation?

www.ingramcontent.com/pod-product-compliance
Lightning Source LLC
Chambersburg PA
CBHW081117080526
44587CB00021B/3641